THE ROYALS

The Royals

FROM THE TURN OF THE 20TH CENTURY TO THE MODERN ROYAL FAMILY

Anna Brett

THE ROYAL FAMILY TREE

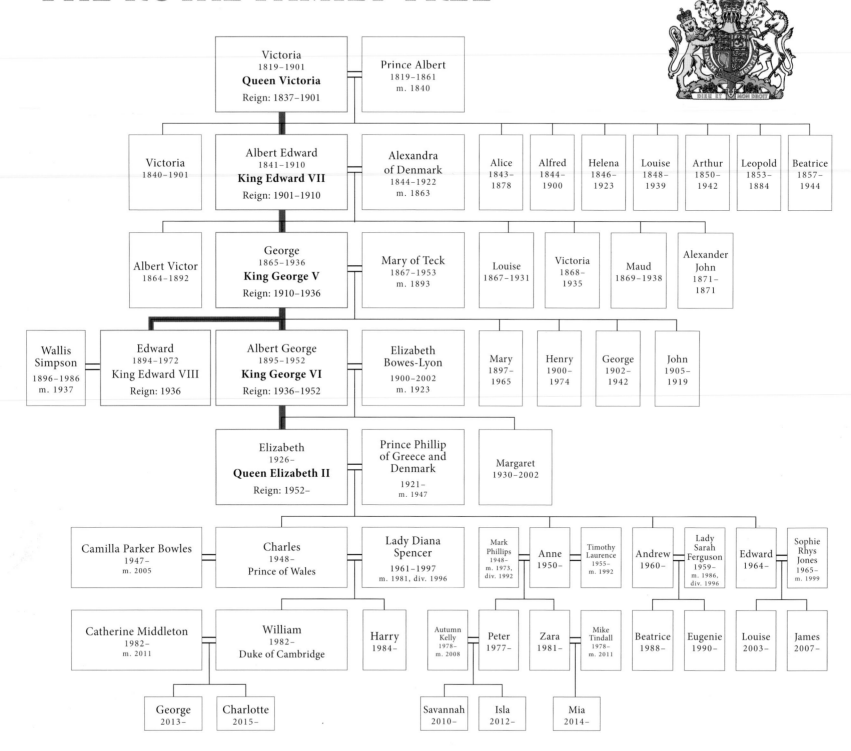

CONTENTS

INTRODUCTION

The Royals

The British Monarchy in the twentieth century has remained a constant in a changing world. This one family, the head of a small nation with a big footprint, has overseen an unimaginable amount of social, political and technological change whilst maintaining the approval of the public they represent. They are a fascinating group of people with a rich history and it is their stability as a family unit that makes them enduring.

Now, living in the twenty first century, we take it for granted that our lives are easily documented through photographs, social media and digital records. Looking back 100 years through our ancestors' documents there are perhaps a handful of photos that exist to show us what their lives looked like. Due to their unique position in society, the royal family is blessed with one of the best collections of high-quality images that document every stage of their lives and the world around them. This book brings over 100 years of royal family visual history together in one place.

Of 26 monarchies around the world, the British Monarchy is arguably the most famous. Although this is in part due to the country's lengthy history and the vast imperial reach of days gone by, it is also due to the characters at the centre of this intriguing story. Whilst kings and queens of the past were strangers to the public, both in appearance and in lifestyle, the twentieth century allowed the common man to establish a public relationship with the head of his country. Monarchs and their families became accessible in a way those at the turn of the century could never have imagined.

Chapters in this photographic record of the past century focus on the reign of five British monarchs and the events that dominated their lives: Edward VII and the golden but short-lived Edwardian Age; George V and the First World War; Edward VIII and his abdication; George VI, the Second World War and the formal establishment of the Commonwealth; Elizabeth II and her vast reign that has brought the country into the modern day. Photos taken throughout Elizabeth II's reign also show the lives of her close family, and include images right up to the present day with Prince George and Princess Charlotte.

Left: Queen Victoria, circa 1869. Known as the 'Grandmother of Europe' she was related to most of the monarchs in Europe at the start of the twentieth century. Her death in 1901 marked the start of a new era for the royals.

Left: Huge crowds gathered outside St Paul's Cathedral as Queen Victoria departed following the Thanksgiving Service on the occasion of her Diamond Jubilee, 2nd June 1897.

Left: King Edward VII in 1906. His reign, although short, oversaw much modernisation of the country and monarchy – both socially and politically.

The British Monarchy's lineage as we know it can be traced back to James I, the King who united England and Scotland. Since 1603 the Houses of Stuart, Hanover and Windsor have provided a stable run of kings and queens for Britain. One of the most prominent British monarchs is Queen Victoria, the woman who brought the country into the twentieth century after 63 years on the throne. Her reign is associated with a great period of development for Britain – there was industrial growth, economic power and a worldwide Empire to watch over. Victoria, however, paved the way for a 'constitutional monarch' – a monarch who has no political power, but whose influence can greatly affect public opinion. When Queen Victoria died in 1901, her popular legacy as well as the changing social attitudes that came with the turn of the new century marked the start of the royals in a new era.

Foreign relations have always been a key part of the monarch's duties, and no more so than in the twentieth century. Two world wars and the changing borders of countries and continents have meant that much of the monarch's job has been to establish or reestablish ties broken by politics. In particular Queen Elizabeth II's foreign relations have been hugely important over the years. In 1965 she visited Germany, the first monarch to do so for 52 years. In 1971 she received Emperor Hirohito of Japan on his first visit to Britain since World War Two. She was the first British sovereign to visit the Middle East in 1979 and 1982 was a historic year as the Pope visited Britain and was received by the monarch for the first time in 450 years. This book documents the royal family's presence abroad as well as at home.

So what does the future hold for the royal family? In recent years a new generation has appeared to produce heirs for the future, so we know the House of Windsor will continue. However, much of their future depends on public approval at home and in the Commonwealth Realms. No one knows what the country will have to deal with over the next century, but as a constitutional staple that has quietly steered the country through two world wars, depression and elation, modernity and controversy, the royal family appears to be well prepared to ride out any difficult times.

Enjoy this record of the twentieth century as seen through the eyes of the royals and uncover the close family that are at the centre of the story.

Left: King George V and Queen Mary at St George's Chapel, Windsor, for the Garter Ceremony, 12th June 1911.

Above: Prince Edward (later King Edward VIII) salutes Anzac (Australia and New Zealand) troops marching through London in 1919.

Above: King George VI and Queen Elizabeth on a visit to Tow Law, a poor mining area in County Durham, February 1939.

Right: Queen Elizabeth II looking through correspondence at her desk in Buckingham Palace, 1959.

Right: A statue of King Edward VII was erected at Pier Head, Liverpool, in 1916. It was commissioned in memory of the popular king and the pose symbolises the duty that comes with being a member of the royal family.

CHAPTER 1
King Edward VII
1901–1910

Albert Edward, or Bertie to his family, was the eldest son of Queen Victoria and titled the Prince of Wales from a very early age. As heir apparent, his parents were keen he be educated strictly to prepare him for taking over the monarchy. However, he was forever in the shadow of his golden father, Albert, and failed to live up to the impossibly high standards set by his mother, Queen Victoria.

After Albert died and Victoria withdrew from public life, the young prince found his calling as a socialite. He lived a life that was not in keeping with how reputable young men had behaved in the past, but through this he endeared himself to the public as a figure whose horses won the high profile races and whose growing waistline gave the papers something to poke fun at.

Edward travelled more than any of his predecessors, he was known as the 'Uncle of Europe' due to his connections – both family and friends – being so extensive. Despite standing in for his mother at state occasions, Queen Victoria heavily restricted his involvement in politics, much to his frustration. Her dislike of his reputation as a 'playboy prince' only served to increase the wedge between mother and son.

Edward found it particularly hard to be excluded from British foreign affairs as he had a vested interest – his older sister became a German Empress and his wife was a Danish Princess. It is telling that as king he was credited for improving relations with France, a feat for which he certainly owed nothing to his mother.

Edward married Alexandra of Denmark in 1863, when he was just 21. It was a match that had been pushed by Victoria and Albert, and although the young couple got on well, Edward had mistresses throughout his life. It is believed that Alexandra was aware of and tolerated these affairs, and they went on to have six children together.

Right: King Edward VII with his wife Queen Alexandra and their grandchildren: Princess Mary, Prince Albert (later King George VI), Prince Henry and Prince Edward (later King Edward VIII), circa 1906.

Left and Right: Edward VII, pictured in about 1875, when he was the Prince of Wales.

18

When Queen Victoria died in 1901, Edward inherited the throne he had waited 59 years for. Domestically, he had a relatively quiet few years, but made it known that he welcomed some of the more liberal measures brought in by the government. However, the constitutional crisis in 1909, when the Conservative dominated House of Lords threw out the Liberal budget and Liberal leader Herbert Asquith called for the reduction in power of the Lords, worried him. He was born and bred as a member of an elite society and the Edwardian era very much represented the golden age of the upper classes. This lifestyle and ruling power was not something Edward was prepared to see overthrown.

Perhaps King Edward VII's greatest achievement was the creation of the *Entente Cordiale* between Britain and France in 1904. After centuries of hostility between the two nations, Edward's charm, grace and goodwill to all men helped ensure the public on both sides of the channel supported the agreement, which ruled out any future wars between the two countries. This proved to be particularly important at a time of growing German dominance.

Edward died in 1910 after a period of bad health. His legacy was a positive one and his reign was a greater success than his mother had surely expected. It is appropriate that the party prince lived his life before World War One would change society forever.

Left: King Edward VII's son, Prince George (later King George V) with his wife Mary and son Prince Edward (later King Edward VIII), 1899.

Right: The future King George V celebrates his birthday with his children on June 3rd, 1902. This photograph includes (l-r) The Duke of York (later King George VI), Princess Mary Countess of Harewood, The Prince of Wales (later King Edward VIII), and The Duke of Gloucester (holding his father's hand).

Left: King Edward VII's grandson Prince Albert (later King George VI) as a child, 1901.

Right: Princess Mary, Prince Edward (later King Edward VIII) and Prince Albert (later King George VI) pose for a portrait, 1902.

Left: King Edward VII and his wife Queen Alexandra in the royal carriage on their way to Olympia in the early 1900s.

Right: King Edward VII, circa 1901, when he succeeded the throne at the age of 59.

24

Left: Queen Alexandra presents Italian runner Pietri Dorando with a consolation gold cup after his disqualification from the London Olympic marathon, 1908. Dorando won the race but had been helped up by umpires after falling down from exhaustion in the final stages.

Right: King Edward VII talking to Wilbur Wright in Le Mans, France, 1909. The aviator, with his brother, is credited with building the first successful airplane.

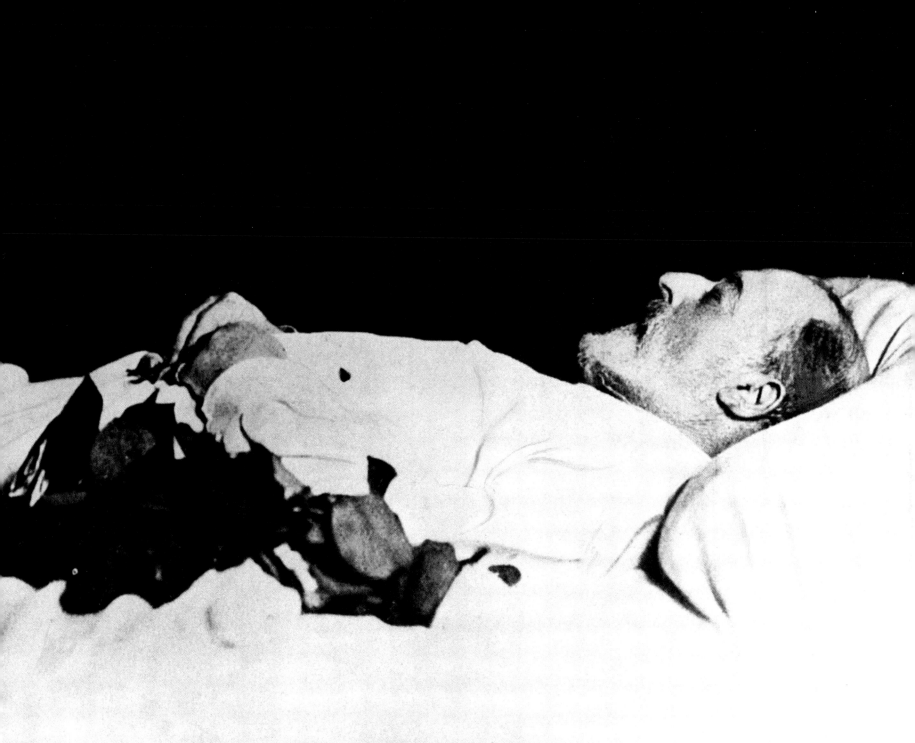

Left: King Edward VII leads in his racehorse Minoru, ridden by jockey Herbert Jones, after winning the Derby at Epsom, June 1909. He was the first reigning British monarch to win a Derby.

Above: King Edward VII died in May 1910 after a series of heart attacks. His body lay in state at Westminster Hall before being taken through the streets of London and on to Windsor by train.

Left and Right: King Edward VII's funeral was held at St George's Chapel, Windsor, May 1910.

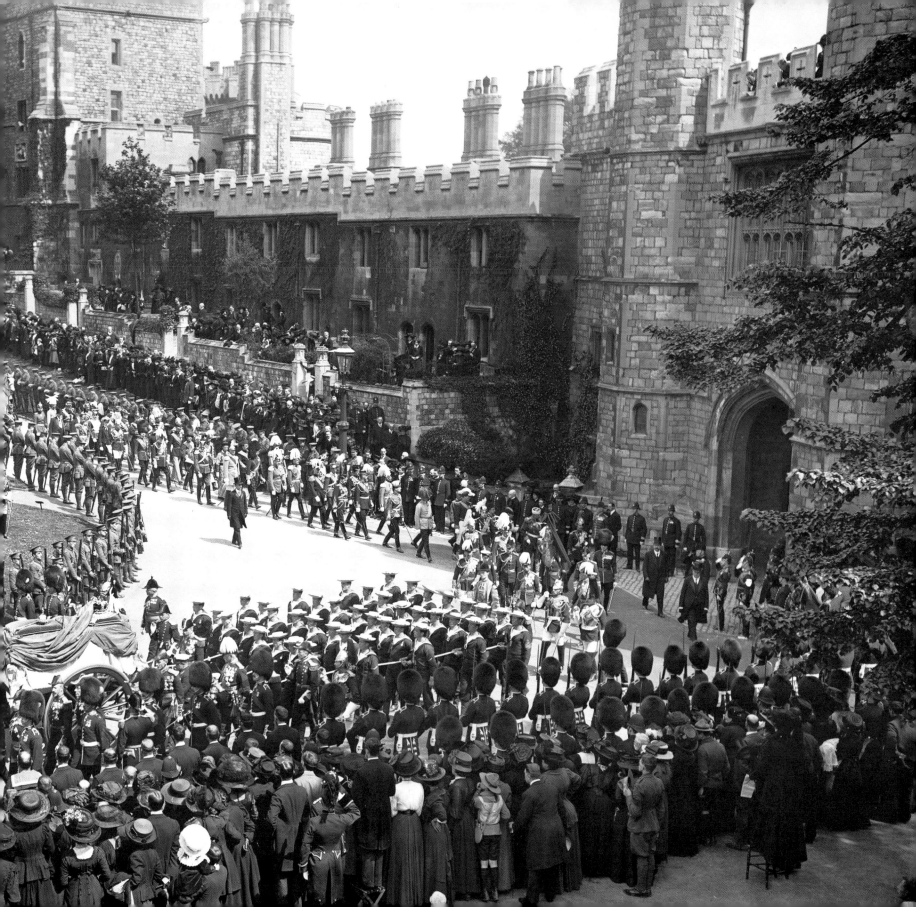

Previous spread: The funeral of King Edward VII, May 1910.

Left: King Edward VII's funeral passing through Windsor, May 1910. There are nine heads of state in this picture.

Right: King George V, his cousin Kaiser Wilhelm II of Germany and The Duke of Connaught (Edward VII's brother) at the funeral, May 1910.

CHAPTER 2
King George V
1910–1936

George V, the second son of Edward VII, became heir to the throne after his brother Albert died from pneumonia as a young adult. Unlike his father, George was not extensively educated and joined the Royal Navy at age 12. He had a close relationship with his father and upon Edward's death George is supposed to have written 'I have lost my best friend and the best of fathers' in his diary. George had been nurtured by his father and was well aware of British politics at home and abroad.

George married Mary of Teck in 1893 and despite her former engagement to his brother, they had a happy marriage and he remained loyal to her. In contrast to his father, George enjoyed a quiet life in the countryside where he and Mary had six children. Nevertheless, as befitting a royal couple, George and Mary did travel extensively – they opened the first Parliament of Australia in 1901 and completed a tour of India in 1905–1906.

When George inherited the throne in 1910 he walked into the constitutional problem his father had been part of. Domestic politics remained turbulent for a few years, and when the Irish question came to the fore, desperate to avoid a civil war, George V gave his blessing to the Home Rule Bill in 1914.

The first years of George's monarchy saw more travel as he and Mary visited Ireland and then India for the Delhi Durbar. The couple were presented as the Emperor and Empress of India and formally oversaw the shift of capital from Calcutta to Delhi. During his time in India George spent many hours game hunting and became known as an expert marksman.

1914 saw the outbreak of World War One and in response to anti-German sentiment from the British public, George looked to cut his ties with his German ancestors. He changed the family name from Saxe-Coburg-Gotha to Windsor and members of the British royal family relinquished their German titles. He spent the war years visiting troops, airfields and factories and provided behind-the-scenes support to the two wartime Prime Ministers, Asquith and Lloyd George.

Left: King George V and Queen Mary visited India in December 1911. The Delhi Durbar was a celebration to mark the succession of the new Emperor of India.

Post-war Europe saw the demise of many monarchies and George's first cousin Tsar Nicholas II and his family were killed in Russia. At home, four years of war had softened social divisions, but not removed them. Socialism spread and the labour movement grew, but with it came positive reforms such as the vote for women over 30. George now ruled over a country where cars were affordable and broadcast radio made the king a more public figure. He delivered the first royal Christmas speech over the radio in 1932.

A year before his death, George V celebrated his Silver Jubilee with celebrations and praise from his public. In 1936 he died at home in the countryside. He was succeeded by his eldest son, Edward, although favoured his second son, Albert, and Albert's young daughter, Elizabeth.

Above: King George V and Queen Mary seen here at the opening of the Festival of Empire at Crystal Palace, 13th May 1911.

Right: King George V inspected a naval guard of honour during a visit to Aberystwyth on the 17th July 1911. The royal party were touring Wales following the investiture of Prince Edward (later King Edward VIII) as the Prince of Wales.

Left: The coronation procession of King George V, 22nd June 1911. The procession is pictured passing through Marble Arch, London.

Above: King George V on horseback reviewing troops in Calcutta during the Delhi Durbar, 1911.

Left: India pays homage to the king and queen during the Delhi Durbar, December 1911.

Right: Suffragette Emily Davidson stepped out in front of racehorse Anmer – owned by King George V – during the 1913 Derby. It is believed that Davidson, one of the most prominent members of the Suffragette Movement, wanted to draw attention to their cause, but she died as a result of her injuries.

Left: King George V, accompanied by his cousin Kaiser Wilhelm II of Germany, is pictured visiting his German Regiment the First Dragoon Guards on a visit to Berlin, 28th May 1913.

Right: King George V and Kaiser Wilhelm II of Germany pictured during the royal visit to Berlin, 1913.

44

IN
REMEMBRANCE
OF
THE GALLANT OFFICERS, N.C.O.s & MEN
OF THE 8 BATT.
DURHAM LIGHT INFANT.
WHO FELL IN AN ATTACK
ON THE
'BUTTE'
DE
WARLENCOURT
NOV 5 & 6
1916

Left: King George V at the Durham light infantry, circa 1915.

Right: King George V describes an incident to King Albert I of Belgium, 25th August 1916.

Left: King George V visited the Western Front in France during World War One in 1917. The photograph shows the king picking up a German helmet.

Above: King George V and Queen Mary in their carriage during the peace celebrations in Hyde Park, London, July 1919.

Left: Queen Alexandra, the widow of Edward VII, unveiled a memorial to nurse Edith Cavell in Trafalgar Square on the 17th March 1920. Edith Cavell was shot for treason by the Germans in the First World War.

Right: Queen Alexandra passed away on 20th November 1925. Her coffin was covered with a purple pall and draped in a standard before lying in state. On guard are two of her servants from Sandringham House.

Left and Right: King George V and Queen Mary arrive for the opening of the parliament of Northern Ireland in Belfast, 23rd June 1921.

Left: The Duke and Duchess of York (later King George VI and Queen Elizabeth) at Victoria Station, London, before leaving for Serbia in October 1923.

Above: The Duke and Duchess of York (later King George VI and Queen Elizabeth) pose with their baby daughter Princess Elizabeth at her christening ceremony at Buckingham Palace surrounded by family members – King George V, Queen Mary, the Duke of Connaught, Princess Mary and the Earl and Countess of Strathmore, May 1926.

Above: King George V is introduced to the Cardiff team by captain Fred
Keenor at the 1927 FA Cup final between Cardiff City and Arsenal.
Cardiff won 1–0 in a historic victory.

Above: King George V in Nottingham greeting West Indian
cricketer L.N. Constantine, July 1928.

Above: King George V and Queen
Mary arrive at Ascot in a horse
drawn carriage with white horses,
June 1931.

Above: Princess Elizabeth (later Queen Elizabeth II) sitting in a horse drawn carriage with her grandparents King George V and Queen Mary on the way back to Balmoral after attending church at nearby Crathie, 5th September 1932.

Above: King George V's silver jubilee was an irresistible marketing opportunity for the railways. While the LNER launched the glamorous *Silver Jubilee* streamlined express, its arch-rival the LMS got the first silver jubilee name, albeit for a more mundane locomotive. Crewe Works craftsmen apply the finish to LMS's *Silver Jubilee* train here in April 1935.

Right: The facade of Selfridges store in Oxford Street, London, was decorated in celebration of the Silver Jubilee of King George V, 4th May 1935.

61

Above: Residents of Campbell Street in Finsbury Park, North London make preparations for King George V's Silver Jubilee celebrations, 3rd May 1935.

Above: King George V died in January 1936. This photo shows the crowds that lined the street around Hyde Park Corner as the funeral procession passed by, 28th January 1936.

Above and Right: The funeral of King George V,
28th January 1936.

Above and Right: The funeral of King
George V, 28th January 1936.

CHAPTER 3
King Edward VIII
January – December 1936

Edward Albert Christian George Andrew Patrick David was born in 1894. He was educated at home and had plans to join the Royal Navy, however he was sent to Oxford University once he became heir to his father's throne. On his 16th birthday, after his father had recently become king, he was invested as Prince of Wales at a ceremony in Wales.

When World War One broke out Edward served in the army and despite being forbidden to visit the front line, he witnessed the horrors of trench warfare. This made him popular with war veterans and from the 1920s onwards he also became popular with the masses. He was quite the celebrity prince as he represented the monarch on various occasions at home and abroad. His good looks brought him much public attention and he was photographed with the leading sportsmen of the time and at key social events.

During his tours around the country, Edward visited the poor and saw the impact of the economic depression in the early 1930s. This further endeared him to the public, however his affairs with married women distanced him from his father. When he began a relationship with an American divorcee, Wallis Simpson, King George V and Queen Mary refused to receive her at Buckingham Palace.

When Edward became king, he generated unease in government circles and took an unorthodox approach to many royal protocols. As it became clear that he intended to marry Wallis, Prime Minster Stanley Baldwin informed him that the marriage would not be acceptable because remarriage after divorce was opposed by the Church of England, which Edward was head of now that he was king.

Left: Edward Prince of Wales (later King Edward VIII) outside the Mansion House in Cardiff, 22nd May 1930.

King Edward VIII had three options in front of him: abandon the idea of marrying Wallis Simpson; marry against the advice of his Prime Minster and cause the government to resign; abdicate the throne and marry. On the 10th December 1936 he signed his abdication papers and on the 11th December announced his decision to abdicate over the radio to a worldwide audience.

Edward left the country and was retitled His Royal Highness The Duke of Windsor by his brother, King George VI. He married Wallis Simpson in June 1937, at a private ceremony in France not attended by the royal family. With the outbreak of World War Two, Edward and Wallis were brought back to Britain but were then posted out to Bermuda in 1940 where Edward was appointed Governor of the Bahamas. At the end of the war the couple returned to France and lived out their lives there with frequent visits to America. They only returned to Britain to attend a handful of royal funerals. Edward did not attend the coronation of Queen Elizabeth II and turned down an invitation to attend Prince Charles' investment as Prince of Wales.

Edward VIII, king for only 325 days and never crowned, died in France in 1972. He was buried at Windsor Castle.

Left: Prince Edward poses for a portrait in his sailor suit, 1902.

Right: Prince Edward and his sister Princess Mary in 1901.

Above: Prince Edward with his
brother and sister in 1901.

Above left: Queen Mary with her sons Prince Edward and Prince Albert, later to become King Edward VIII and King George VI.

Above right: Prince Edward with famed cricketer W. G. Grace, circa 1900.

Left: Prince Edward at his investiture as the Prince of Wales, Caernarfon Castle, Wales, 13th July 1911.

Right: George V and Queen Mary with their son Prince Edward on the occasion of his investiture as Prince of Wales.

Left: Prince Edward during a visit to the Curran Munitions Works in Cardiff, February 1918.

Right: Lady Astor greeting Prince Edward at Plymouth on his return from the Eastern Tour, June 1922.

Left: Prince Edward and his brother Prince Albert (later King George VI) pictured on their way to the international rugby match between Wales and Ireland at Cardiff Arms Park, 8th March 1924.

Left: Prince Edward presents a cup to Cliff Porter, captain of the New Zealand rugby union team, 22nd January 1925. The team were nicknamed the 'Invincibles' as they won all 32 games on their 1924–25 tour.

Right: Prince Edward with his brother Prince Albert at the Stock Exchange in London, circa 1925.

Above and Right: Prince Edward visits Durham on Tyneside, 29th January 1929. He is pictured among miners' families in a typical courtyard surrounded by pitmen's dwellings. His public appearances made him increasingly popular with the masses.

Left: A woman holding a banner outside the Houses of Parliament during King Edward VIII's abdication crisis, December 1936. The banner reads: "Hands Off Our King. Abdication means revolution".

Above: Crowds gather outside Buckingham Palace waiting for news of King Edward VIII's abdication, December 1936. The constitutional crisis was caused by Edward VIII's wish to marry divorced American Mrs Wallis Simpson.

Prince Albert, soon to be King George VI, during the abdication crisis, December 1936.

Left: King Edward VIII was renamed the Duke of Windsor after his abdication. He and his new wife, the Duchess of Windsor arrived in England again in September 1939 after the outbreak of war.

Above: The Duchess of Windsor, Wallis Simpson.

Right: Edward, Duke of Windsor, was desperate for a role in the war effort but the British government posted him to the Bahamas to avoid risk of capture by the Germans.

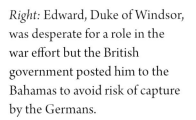

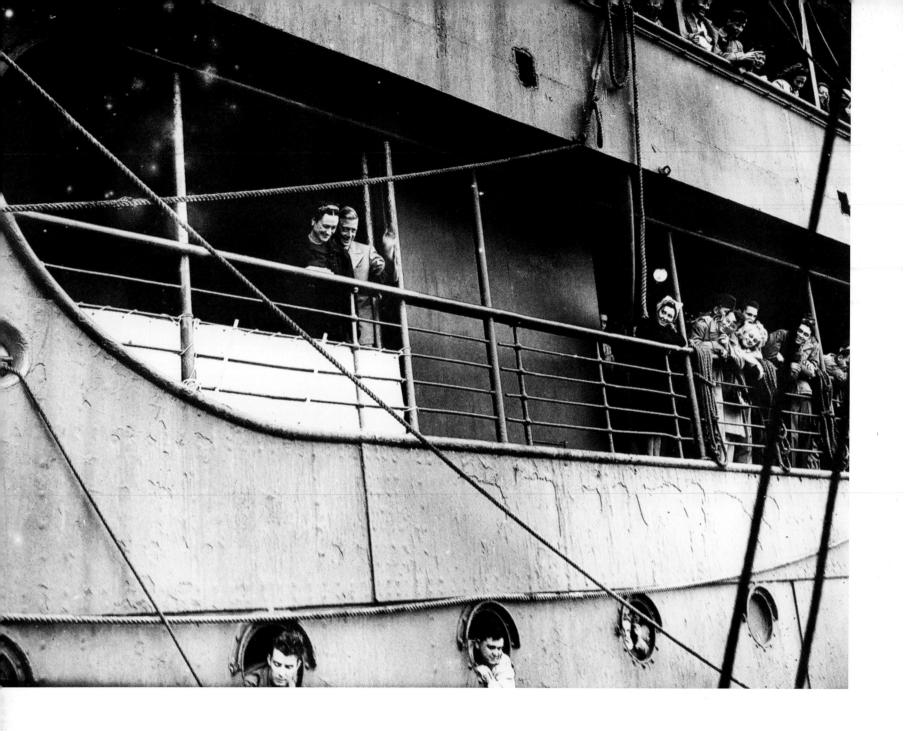

Above: The Duke and Duchess of Windsor aboard the ship *Argentina* in Plymouth, September 1945.

Right: The Duke and Duchess of Windsor with their dogs, Trooper and Disry, by the marble fireplace in the library of their home in Paris, 24th July 1955. The portrait of the Duchess is by the American painter Preaul Brockhurst.

CHAPTER 4

King George VI

1936–1952

King George VI was born Albert Frederick Arthur George in 1895. As second son to George V and his wife Mary, he was not expected to inherit the throne. He served in the Royal Navy during World War One and then joined the Royal Air Force. In 1923 he married Lady Elizabeth Bowes-Lyon and Princess Elizabeth was born in 1926, followed by Princess Margaret in 1930.

After the unexpected abdication of his brother Edward, George was proclaimed king on the 12th December 1936. His coronation took place in 1937. George was a reluctant king and he spoke with a stammer which made public speaking difficult for him. However, he took up his role with determination and support from his wife, and chose to rule with the name George to emphasize the link with his father. With the support of a voice coach he also went on to frequently address the nation over the radio.

During his first years of reign he visited France and supported Prime Minster Chamberlain's appeasement of Germany. He made a historic visit to the United States in 1939 – the first reigning monarch to set foot in the country. The short visit did wonders to build American support for Britain as Europe approached a second world war.

When Britain declared war on Germany in 1939, King George decided to keep his family in London. They shared the same wartime experiences as the common man as Buckingham Palace was bombed and the family were subject to rationing. George and Elizabeth toured the country to help boost morale and George formed a strong relationship with Prime Minster Winston Churchill. The king become a symbol for strong British resistance. When the war ended in 1945, the royal family appeared on the balcony of Buckingham Palace alongside Churchill, gaining huge public approval.

King George's wartime legacy was the creation of the George Cross for acts of heroism or courage when not under direct enemy fire. He wanted to mark the bravery of those civilians experiencing the war through events such as the Blitz in London. George also awarded the George Cross to Malta for the bravery shown by the country during the war.

Left: Portrait of the Duke and Duchess of York with their daughters Princesses Elizabeth and Margaret in the 1930s, before the couple became King George VI and Queen Elizabeth.

George VI's reign was dominated by the war but he also oversaw the demise of the British Empire. He was the last Emperor of India and in 1947 the territory was divided into India and Pakistan. Countries formerly in the Empire were recognized as members of the modern Commonwealth in 1949; they shared language and culture but were all free states with no obligation to each other. The monarch was appointed Head of the Commonwealth and remains a monarch to 16 member states, known as Commonwealth Realms.

George's health deteriorated after the war – a heavy smoker throughout his life he had to have a lung removed and many felt he never recovered from the stresses of the war. He died in 1952.

Left: Prince Albert (later King George VI) age six in 1901.

Right: Elizabeth Bowes-Lyon
(later Queen Elizabeth) as a child.

Above: Elizabeth Bowes-Lyon in the 1920s.

Above: Elizabeth Bowes-Lyon in 1923.

Elizabeth leaving for her wedding
to Prince Albert, April 1923.

Left: The Duke and Duchess of York visit Belfast, 1924.

Right: The Duke and Duchess of York arrive for shooting season at Glamis, Scotland, 1926.

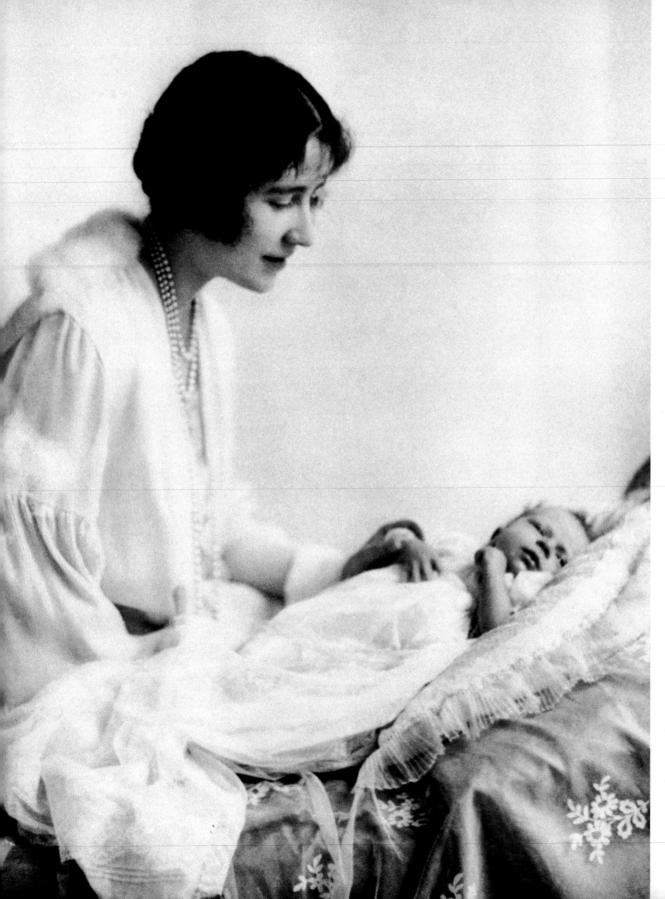

Left: The Duchess of York with her daughter Elizabeth (later Queen Elizabeth II), 1926.

Right: Elizabeth, Duchess of York, graces the footplate of Southern Railway's brand new premier express locomotive – No. 850 Lord Nelson – at Ashford Locomotive Works, Kent, on 21st October 1926.

Left: The Duke and Duchess of York arrive in Sydney Australia, May 1927.

Right: The Duchess of York amongst crowds, November 1929.

Above: The Duchess of York arrives at the Royal Tournament at Olympia, with her daughters Princess Elizabeth and Princess Margaret, circa 1933.

Above: Elizabeth, Duchess of York, with daughters Princess Elizabeth and Princess Margaret, 1935.

Above: The Duke and Duchess of York with their daughter Elizabeth, circa 1934.

Left: The coronation of King George VI took place on the 12th May 1937. This aerial view shows the procession in progress marching down Victoria Street towards Westminster Abbey.

Right: The coronation itself took place inside Westminster Abbey.

Above: The procession outside Westminster Abbey.

Left: King George VI's procession makes its way through Cumberland gate into Hyde Park on its return journey to Buckingham Palace as thousands of people cheer from the side of the road.

Above: The *Daily Mirror* newspaper on Saturday 15th May 1937 shows King George VI and his family in the official Royal Coronation Portrait.

Right: The Gold State Coach carrying King George VI passes through Marble Arch on its way back to Buckingham Palace.

Left: Big Ben and late night revellers in London following the coronation of King George VI.

Right: King George VI and Queen Elizabeth at Royal Ascot in June 1937. It is tradition for the king and queen to arrive by horse and carriage along the racecourse.

Left: Queen Elizabeth and King George VI in Scotland with local women, 1937.

Right: King George VI and Queen Elizabeth at the Chelsea Flower Show in 1938.

Left: The Duke and Duchess of York, with four Canadian Mounted Police who were their personal body guards during their Canadian tour in June 1939.

Left: King George VI and Queen Elizabeth in Canada, 1939. The are walking down the crowded roadway to the University of Toronto where Queen Elizabeth presented Colours to the Toronto Scottish Regiment. The roadway was lined by Cadets of the University Cadet Corps.

Above: King George VI and Queen Elizabeth arrive at Southampton at the end of their important tour of the USA and Canada, 1939.

Above: King George VI and Queen Elizabeth visit the Tow Low Social Service Centre, 23rd February 1939.

Above: Queen Elizabeth and King George VI with Princess Margaret at Crathie Church, 1939.

Left: World War II began in September 1939. King George VI visited Coventry on the 16th November 1940 and spent four hours sharing in the city's sorrow as he walked through the bombed streets, covered with mud and rubble, to meet the people that had been in the middle of the blitz. He is seen here in the cathedral ruins.

Right: King George VI walks past a wrecked car on a walkabout in the East End of London following a Nazi air raid, 10th September 1940.

Left: King George VI visits the bomb damaged city of Bristol following an air raid in December 1940.

Left: King George VI inspects firemen on his visit to Birmingham after a bombing raid, December 1940.

Right: Queen Mary, mother of King George VI, had her own part to play during the war. Here she can be seen inspecting a line of Air Raid Wardens.

Left: Princess Elizabeth as Junior Commander in the ATS inspecting The Motor Transport Training Centre at Camberley, Surrey, during the Second World War, 1945.

Right: VE Day celebrations in London at the end of the Second World War. King George VI with Prime Minister Winston Churchill, Ernest Bevin, Herbert Morrison and other members of cabinet and chiefs of staff in the grounds of Buckingham Palace, 8th May 1945.

VE Day celebrations in London at the end of the Second World War, 8th May 1945. Prime Minister Winston Churchill joins Princess Elizabeth, Queen Elizabeth, King George VI and Princess Margaret on the balcony of Buckingham Palace during the celebrations in central London.

Huge crowds gathered outside Buckingham Palace
during the celebrations, 8th May 1945.

Above: Queen Elizabeth and George VI visit Caernarfon, Wales, 1946.
Scouts and guides line the steps either side of them.

Right: Princess Margaret, Princess Elizabeth and their mother Queen Elizabeth at a garden party in Durban during their visit to South Africa in 1947.

Left: Princess Elizabeth and her father King George VI leave the Royal Box for the paddock at the end of the Epsom Derby in June 1948.

Right: George VI died on the 6th February 1952. Three Queens are pictured here watching as his body is placed in Westminster Abbey: Queen Elizabeth II, Queen Mary and Queen Elizabeth. Over 300,000 people visited the Great Hall at Westminster where the King's body lay in state.

CHAPTER 5

Queen Elizabeth II

1952–

Queen Elizabeth II was born on the 21st April 1926 in London. The first child of The Duke and Duchess of York, she was third in line to the throne but never expected to reign. She was christened Elizabeth Alexandra Mary and in 1930 gained a sister, Margaret Rose. The family were close and lived a relatively quiet life in London, until 1936 when King George V died. That same year King Edward VIII decided to abdicate and Elizabeth's father became king. Aged just 11, Elizabeth attended her father's coronation knowing she was next in line for the throne. Her life had changed forever.

Princess Elizabeth was educated at home and focus was put on subjects that would prepare her for her future role as Head of the Church of England and Monarch of Britain and the Commonwealth. Aged 21, in July 1947, Elizabeth's engagement to Philip Mountbatten was announced and they were married five months later. Prince Charles was born in 1948 and became heir apparent. Princess Anne was then born in 1950.

In 1952 Elizabeth stood in for her father on a tour to Australia and New Zealand with a stop in Africa on route. However, they never made it further than Kenya, as word reached the royal party that King George VI had died. Elizabeth returned to Britain as Queen Elizabeth II. Her coronation took place on 2nd June 1953 and was broadcast on radio and television to hundreds of thousands of people around the world. This global transmission truly marked the start of the royal family in the modern era.

The new queen approached her role with enthusiasm and dedication; in the first ten years she travelled extensively to all corners of the United Kingdom and Commonwealth. She established her mark on royal traditions and oversaw Parliament and the start of many prime minsters to serve under her.

After eight years on the throne, Queen Elizabeth II gave birth to Prince Andrew, the first child born to a reigning monarch since 1857. In 1964 Prince Edward arrived. This family orientated queen decided to make herself more accessible to the public than ever before – in 1969 a TV documentary was made about her and the family and in 1970 she and the Duke of Edinburgh

Left: Princess Elizabeth and the Duke of Edinburgh arm in arm,
28th November 1947.

began the practice of 'the walkabout' when on tour to allow them to meet and chat to members of the public.

The Queen's third decade of service saw her 25th wedding anniversary and her Silver Jubilee. The country celebrated with a public holiday, street parties and a thanksgiving service in St Paul's Cathedral. She also became a grandmother for the first time in 1977.

The fourth decade of Elizabeth's reign was marked by the British Forces involvement in the Falklands War and the Gulf War. The royal family has always had a strong link to the forces and Elizabeth and Philip experienced first hand the concern for the safety of troops abroad as Prince Andrew served in the Falklands.

Her fifth decade on the throne brought the nation into a new millennium and constitutional history was made with the devolution of power for Scotland and Wales. Sadly this decade also saw a fire at Windsor Castle, the death of Princess Diana, and the September 11th terrorist attacks in America that would profoundly affect the entire world.

Upon reaching her Golden Jubilee, the year of 2002 was also tinged with personal sadness for the Queen as both her sister and mother passed away. However, a year of celebration was marked with yet more travel and the spread of goodwill.

Now in her seventh decade on the throne, Queen Elizabeth II matches Queen Victoria's record reign of 63 years. The three generations of family below her are becoming more involved in royal affairs and help share her duties, but at almost 90 years of age Queen Elizabeth still looks to be as dedicated, interested and loyal to her subjects as ever before.

Left: Princess Elizabeth dances arms linked with Lady Pamela Mountbatten and the Duke of Edinburgh during an eightsome reel at The Saddle Club Dance, Malta.

Above: Princess Elizabeth married the Duke of Edinburgh on the 20th November 1947. Here she arrives at Westminster Abbey with her father King George VI.

Left: Princess Elizabeth and the Duke of Edinburgh's official wedding day picture, 20 November 1947.

Right: The wedding party pictured in Buckingham Palace, 20th November 1947. Front row, left to right: Queen Mary, Princess Andrew of Greece, the bridegroom's mother, the pages – Prince William of Gloucester, and Prince Michael of Kent, The King and Queen, Dowager Marchioness of Milford Haven. Second row, left to right: four bridesmaids: The Hon Margaret Elphinstone, Lady Pamela Mountbatten, Lady Mary Cambridge and Princess Alexandra, the groomsman: David Mountbatten Marquess of Milford Haven, the other four bridesmaids: Princess Margaret, Lady Caroline Montagu-Douglas-Scott, Lady Elizabeth Lambart and Miss Diana Bowes-Lyon.

Left: Prince Charles, pictured in the arms of his mother, Princess Elizabeth after his christening on 15th December 1948 at Buckingham Palace.

Right: Princess Elizabeth and her husband Prince Philip with their two children Prince Charles and Princess Anne, circa 1951.

Above: The Coronation of Queen Elizabeth II, 2nd June 1953. She was crowned Queen of the United Kingdom, Canada, Australia, New Zealand, South Africa, Ceylon and Pakistan, as well as taking on the role of Head of the Commonwealth.

Above: Queen Elizabeth II's Coronation, 1953. The Duke of Edinburgh kneels in homage to his wife, the new queen.

Left: A brightly decorated trolleybus at the Pier Head, South Shields, for the 1953 coronation of Queen Elizabeth II.

Above: A street party on Saville Road, Blackpool for the coronation day, 2nd June 1953.

Above: Residents of St Pauls Road, Islington, celebrating the coronation of Queen Elizabeth.

Right: A procession of royal and other representatives of foreign states is seen here making its way down Northumberland Avenue ahead of the Gold State Coach carrying the Queen to Westminster Abbey for her coronation.

Left: Crowds watch the coronation procession in London.

Right: The Gold State Coach at Admiralty Arch, during the procession.

Left: The royal family in their robes after the Coronation. Back Row: The Duke of Gloucester, The Duke of Edinburgh and The Duke of Kent. Front Row: Princess Alexandra, Prince Michael of Kent, Princess Anne, Princess Marina, Princess Margaret, The Queen, The Queen Mother, Princess Royal, The Duchess of Gloucester with Prince William and Prince Richard of Gloucester.

Above: Prince Charles looking bored with his chin on his hand between the Queen Mother and Princess Margaret in the Royal Box at Westminster Abbey.

Left: Queen Elizabeth with Prince Philip, Prince Charles and Princess Anne on the balcony of Buckingham Palace after the coronation.

Above: The royal family on the balcony at Buckingham Palace.

Left: Queen Elizabeth II making her Christmas Day broadcast from Government House, Auckland, New Zealand, in 1953.

Right: Queen Elizabeth II and her husband Prince Philip, the Duke of Edinburgh, on their Mediterranean tour in May 1954.

Left: Queen Elizabeth II inspects a mounted guard of honour in Sydney, Australia, 1954.

Right: Queen Elizabeth II and Prince Philip say goodbye to Lieutenant General Sir Charles and Lady Gairdner and Prime Minister Menzies in Fremantle, Australia before boarding the *Gothic* for the Voyage to Ceylon, 1954.

Left: Queen Elizabeth II visits Tasmania, Australia, in March 1954. She made a regal entry to the Hobart City Hall for the Civic Ball.

Right: Princess Anne (aged 4) and Prince Charles (aged 6) walk through Green Park with their Governess on their return to Buckingham Palace after visiting their grandmother at Clarence House in November 1954. Visitors to the park were unaware of the royal children who were enjoying a little freedom. They were escorted from a distance by one royal bodyguard.

Left: The Prince of Wales with his sister Princess Anne at the door of a railway train in Aberdeen station.

Right: Prince Charles and Princess Anne are pictured with their uncle Lord Mountbatten on the Island of Malta, April 1954.

Queen Elizabeth II and Prince Philip pose for a photograph on the main deck of HMS *Glasgow* with the ship's crew, May 1954.

Queen Elizabeth II visits
Sheffield in the North of
England, October 1954.

Left: Queen Elizabeth II, the Queen Mother, Prince Charles and Princess Anne attend a polo match at Windsor, June 1955.

Right: Queen Elizabeth II with Prince Philip are welcomed to Gateshead with the majestic backdrop of the Tyne Bridge.

Left: The Queen and the Duke of Edinburgh on the royal train as it leaves Lagos terminus, on route for Ibadan, February 1956. They were on a royal tour of Nigeria.

Right: American film actress Marilyn Monroe meets Queen Elizabeth II at the Royal Command Film Performance at Leicester Square in London, 29th October 1956.

Above: When Queen Elizabeth II visited Tynemouth the crowds used *Evening Chronicle* and *The Journal* posters to welcome her.

Above: The Queen chats with Capt. A.C. Farquharson of Invercauld whilst the Marquess of Aberdeen speaks to the Duke of Edinburgh, September 1956. The Marquess is Lord Lieutenant of Aberdeenshire and Chief of the Braemar Games.

Above: Queen Elizabeth II leading in her horse Carrogan into the enclosure after the horse's victory in the Oaks race at Epsom, 7th June 1957.

Right: Queen Elizabeth II and her mother at the Badminton Horse Trials carrying her Dachshund dog.

Left: Queen Elizabeth II during her visit to Canada, June 1959.

Right: Queen Elizabeth welcomed President Eisenhower and his wife when they arrived by air at the Royal Canadian Air Force base at St Hubert, near Montreal, June 1959.

CHAPTER 6
The Royal Family
1960–1979

This period of Queen Elizabeth's reign was marked by the birth of Andrew and Edward and the growth of her family. Like any young family at this time they had to balance a busy lifestyle with the changing attitudes of society.

Around the world, British and American culture was influencing a generation. American President, John F. Kennedy and his wife Jackie were celebrities in their own right and British group The Beatles became the first global pop-rock band. While Britain wasn't involved, the Vietnam War sparked huge debate around the world and student movements linked to the war gave the youth of the decade a loud voice in society. In Britain, the death of Winston Churchill in 1965 marked the end of a difficult 50 years for the country and he was given a full state funeral with representatives from nations around the world attending, including, unusually for a politician's funeral, the Queen.

Prince Charles and Princess Anne became young adults during this period of social change and had to forge an identity for themselves as royals. Charles studied abroad in Australia for a period before gaining a degree from Cambridge. Anne married Mark Phillips at age 23 and went on to have two children. Princess Margaret also had two children in the 1960s and life around Queen Elizabeth II was filled with the optimism of youth.

The documentary 'Royal Family' was commissioned by the Queen and aired in 1969. It was intended to show that the royals were like most other families, and included behind-the-scenes footage of their life at Buckingham Palace and at work around the world. However, unlike any normal family, the year also saw the investiture of Charles as Prince of Wales and he was crowned by the Queen in a televised ceremony.

In the 1970s Charles embarked on a military career and served in the Navy and Air Force. He was an eligible young bachelor and was linked to many young women during this period, including Camilla Shand whom he would later marry in 2005. Much media attention was given to his female friendships, although it was made clear that his choice of wife, and thus the future

Left: Queen Elizabeth II and her husband Prince Philip in a happy mood during their visit to Bathurst in the West African country of Gambia, December 1961.

queen, should be one that both the royals and the government approved of.

In 1977 Queen Elizabeth II marked her Silver Jubilee with celebrations around the country and Commonwealth. She spent the actual weekend with her family at Windsor, but the summer was given over to festivities. It is estimated that The Queen and Duke of Edinburgh travelled 56,000 miles over this one celebratory year. The Queen, grounded as ever, took the opportunity of this attention to stress the unity of the nation and reaffirmed her pledge to give her life in service to the British people.

Left: Queen Elizabeth II and her husband Prince Philip with their children Princess Anne, Prince Charles and baby Prince Andrew on his first holiday to Balmoral, 8th September 1960.

Above: The Prince of Wales pictured with his grandmother, The Queen Mother, sister Princess Anne and brother Prince Andrew, in the garden of Clarence House, August 1960. The royal children helped their grandmother unpack her 60th birthday presents.

Above: The Duke of Edinburgh, Jackie Kennedy, Queen Elizabeth and
American President Kennedy at Buckingham Palace, 6th June 1961.

Left: Queen Elizabeth II and husband Prince Philip are pictured at a durbar at Bo, Sierra Leone, in November 1961.

Left: The Prince of Wales at Gordonstoun School, in step with his father the Duke of Edinburgh. Bringing up the rear is Captain Iain Tennant, Chairman of the Board of Governors.

Right: The Prince of Wales with his sister Princess Anne at the top of aircraft steps in London before his departure to Timbertop School in Australia.

Left: The Prince of Wales with his sister, Princess Anne, as they leave Buckingham Palace by coach to attend the opening of Parliament by the Queen the first time.

Above: Prince Andrew running at Smith Lawn in Windsor, July 1965.

Left: Princess Margaret with husband Lord Snowden and baby son David Armstrong-Jones, November 1961.

Right: Princess Margaret with American President Lyndon B. Johnson at the White House in Washington, D.C., November 1965.

Left: Princess Margaret meets The Beatles at the Royal Variety Show in November 1963. The Beatles are, left to right, Ringo Starr, John Lennon, George Harrison and Paul McCartney.

Right: Queen Elizabeth II walking purposefully across a polo pitch, June 1965.

Left: Winston Churchill's State Funeral took place on the 30th January 1965. Few bouquets of flowers have ever carried such enormous weight. Queen Elizabeth II made this one small gesture that spoke volumes as the nation and the Commonwealth were united in grief over the death of a much loved statesman and leader.

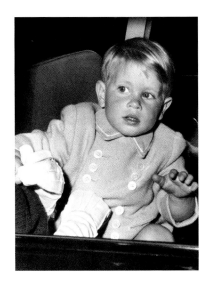

Above: Prince Edward aged two, sitting on his nanny's lap waving as he goes to visit Princess Anne in hospital, May 1966.

Right: Queen Elizabeth II, with Princes Edward and Andrew, leaves Euston Station by car after returning from holiday at Balmoral, 1960.

Left: Queen Elizabeth presents the Jules Rimet trophy to England captain Bobby Moore after the World Cup Final football match at Wembley Stadium, 30th July 1966. England beat West Germany 4–2 after extra time.

Right: The Queen and Prince Philip visiting Aberfan, Wales, 29th October 1966.

Left: Princess Anne accompanied by Prince Edward driving a French Chaise, June 1969.

Right: Prince Edward at five years old, August 1969.

Above: Queen Elizabeth with her family at Windsor Castle, 20th April 1968.

Above: Prince Charles pictured with the rest of the royal children on the East Terrace at Windsor Castle on Christmas Day after the morning service in St George's Chapel, 1969. The children are, left to right, Master James Ogilvy, Lady Sarah Armstrong-Jones, The Earl of St Andrews, Lady Helen Windsor, The Prince of Wales, Viscount Linley, Prince Andrew, Miss Marina Ogilvy, Princess Anne and Prince Edward.

Left: Princess Anne and Princess Alice arriving at the Warner Theatre, November 1969.

Right: The Queen opening the Victoria Line in the London tube network, 10th March 1969.

Left: Prince Charles wearing military uniform in public for the first time at inauguration ceremony of the new Royal Regiment of Wales, June 1969.

Above: The Queen and Prince Philip on board a private jet, 1969. This image is taken from the BBC & ITV co-production documentary, the 'Royal Family' which was first transmitted on 21st June 1969. The documentary gave audiences an unprecedented view of a year in the private and public life of The Queen and her family.

Left: The Queen, Prince Philip and Prince Charles visiting President Nixon, 1969.

Right: View from Caernarfon Castle across the town square during the Investiture of Prince Charles as The Prince of Wales, 1st July 1969.

Left: Queen Elizabeth II and Prince Charles walk towards Queen Eleanor's Gate during the Investiture procession, 1st July 1969.

Right: Queen Elizabeth II places the crown on the head of Prince Charles during his Investiture as Prince of Wales at Caernarfon.

Left: Queen Elizabeth II presents her son Prince Charles to the people of Wales as they stand at Queen Eleanor's Gate.

Right: Queen Elizabeth II and Prince Charles leaving Caernarfon Castle after the Investiture ceremony.

Left: The Queen with the Duchess of Windsor and the Duke of Edinburgh at Windsor Castle for the funeral of Edward VIII, 5th June 1972.

Left: Queen Elizabeth II seen here with the Queen Mother and Prince Edward during their summer tour of the Scottish Islands, November 1972.

Right: The Queen and Prince Philip celebrated their Silver Wedding anniversary with their family in November 1972.

Left: The wedding of Princess Anne to Captain Mark Phillips at St Paul's Cathedral, November 1973.

Right: Princess Anne and Captain Mark Phillips leaving Westminster Abbey, November 1973.

Right: The royal family with King Carl Gustav of Sweden during his State Visit, July 1975. Here they are at a State Banquet in Holyrood House – right to left, Duke of Gloucester, Princess Margaret, Prince Charles, Earl Mountbatten (not visible), Queen Elizabeth II, King Carl Gustav, Mr John Ambler, The Queen Mother, Princess Margaretta of Sweden and Prince Philip.

Left: Princess Alice, Countess of Athlone, in March 1978. The 95-year-old princess was the last surviving granddaughter of Queen Victoria.

Above: Bob Willis shakes hands with The Queen before a game of cricket, 12th March 1977. The Centenary Test match between Australia and England was held at the Melbourne Cricket Ground, Australia.

Right: Queen Elizabeth II takes a stroll in the grounds of Balmoral Castle with Prince Philip, Prince Charles, Prince Andrew, Prince Edward and Princess Anne with her son Peter Phillips, November 1979.

Above: The royal family attending the funeral of Queen Elizabeth's uncle Lord Mountbatten, the Earl of Burma, 1979.

Right: Queen Elizabeth II, The Queen Mother, Prince Philip, Prince Charles, Prince Andrew and Prince Edward walk to their seats at the funeral.

Queen Elizabeth II with her husband Prince Philip and sons Prince Edward, Prince Charles and Prince Andrew in October 1979.

CHAPTER 7

The Changing Royal Family

1980–1997

Prince Charles met Lady Diana Spencer in the late 1970s and had proposed to her by February 1981. Their marriage in July 1981 marked the start of a new focus for the general public in relation to the royals. Diana gave Charles the glamour he had previously lacked. Their 'fairytale' wedding was televised to hundreds of millions of people around the world and took place in St Paul's Cathedral rather than Westminster Abbey to allow for more space and a longer procession route through London. Diana's dress, now famous for it's voluptuous style and 25ft long train, was designed by Elizabeth and David Emanuel and became a visual icon of the era. Charles wore his full naval uniform. As is tradition, Charles and Diana appeared on the balcony of Buckingham Palace and raised a cheer from the crowds when they kissed. They spent their honeymoon in Hampshire before going on a cruise around the Mediterranean. When they returned to Britain they went to Balmoral to join the rest of the royal family and the press were given an exclusive photo opportunity with the newlyweds.

Prince William was born in 1982 and Harry followed in 1984. However the fairytale was not to last and after just five years of marriage the strain of Charles and Diana's relationship began to show publicly. In 1992 their separation was formally announced in Parliament. They divorced in 1996.

In the mid 1980s another romance was blossoming as Prince Andrew formed a strong relationship with Sarah Ferguson. They married in 1986 in Westminster Abbey. Two daughters followed in 1988 and 1990 – Beatrice and Eugenie. While they appeared to be a happy couple, they too separated in 1992 and divorced in 1996.

Left: Princess Diana and Prince Charles after their wedding ceremony, 29th July 1981. There were 3,500 people in the congregation at St Paul's Cathedral, London.

Diana, although no longer with Charles, endeared herself to the public through her humanitarian work and she fought hard to shelter the upbringing of Princes William and Harry so they could try to lead lives that were not in full view of the world. Diana, however, was not afforded such luxury and was famously hounded by the media.

Tragically, Diana was killed in a car crash in Paris in 1997. She was with her close friend, Dodi Fayed, who was also killed. Public grief was unprecedented and scenes of a sea of flowers left outside Kensington Palace were beamed around the world. The public felt they had lost their fairytale princess.

The royal family was criticized at this time for their rigid adherence to protocol, formality was frowned upon at a time when the most popular royal had been the one who did not have blood ties. The media was also criticized for its unending pursuit of Diana and rules were put in place to protect the grieving princes. One of the most poignant images of this time is of that of William and Harry walking behind their mother's coffin on its procession through London. Their raw grief masked by royal pageantry.

Above: Prince Charles with his brother Prince Andrew, July 1980.

Below: The Queen Mother attending the Garter Ceremony at Windsor Castle, June 1980.

Left: Queen Elizabeth II, The Queen Mother and Prince Charles at Sandown Park, March 1980.

Left: Prince Charles with his fiancée Lady Diana Spencer after announcing their engagement, February 1981.

Right: Prince Charles and Lady Diana Spencer at Balmoral, May 1981.

Left: Lady Diana Spencer arrives at St Paul's Cathedral with her father Earl Spencer for her marriage to Prince Charles, 29th July 1981.

Right: Prince Charles and Princess Diana after the ceremony.

227

Left: Princess Diana and Prince Charles walking down the isle being watched by both families after their wedding ceremony.

Above: Prince Charles and Princess Diana drive in an open carriage to Buckingham Palace after their marriage ceremony at St Pauls.

Above: Charles and Diana
with Queen Elizabeth II and
Prince Philip on the balcony at
Buckingham Palace after their
marriage ceremony.

Above: The royal couple with their bridal attendants on balcony of Buckingham Palace. From left to right: India Hicks (aged 13), Edward van Cutsem (aged 8), Princess Diana, Prince Charles, Clementine Hambro (aged 5), Lord Nicholas Windsor (aged 11), Sarah-Jane Gaselee (aged 11), Lady Sarah Armstrong-Jones (aged 17), Catherine Cameron (aged 6).

Left: Charles and Diana arriving at Buckingham Palace after their wedding.

Right: Prince Charles and Princess Diana standing together on board a ship to start their honeymoon, 1981.

Left: Prince Charles kissing the hand of Princess Diana after their honeymoon at Balmoral in Scotland, 1981.

Right: Prince Charles and Princess Diana on board the Royal Yacht *Britannia* whilst on honeymoon.

Left: Charles and Diana happy and in love at Balmoral after their honeymoon.

Right: Charles and Diana at Balmoral.

Above: The Queen and family on the balcony at Buckingham Palace
following the Trooping of the Colour ceremony, 15th June 1981.

Right: Princess Diana at the Braemar Games in Scotland with Prince Charles, Queen Elizabeth II and The Queen Mother laughing with Geoff Capes, September 1981.

Right: Prince Charles and Princess Diana, September 1981.

Left: The Prince and Princess of Wales attending the polo at Smith's Lawn, Windsor, 2nd May 1982.

Above: Crowds gather outside the gate of Buckingham Palace to read the official announcement of the birth of Prince William to the Prince and Princess of Wales, 21st June 1982.

Right: The official announcement of the birth of Prince William pinned to the gates of Buckingham Palace, 21st June 1982.
The announcement reads:
"Her Royal Highness The Princess of Wales was safely delivered of a son at 9.03pm today."

Left and Right: Princess Diana holds her son Prince William in her arms in the White Drawing Room of Buckingham Palace following a private christening ceremony in the Music Room, 4th August 1982.

244

Left: Prince William's christening, official photo, 4th August 1982.

Right: The Queen Mother holding Prince William at the infant's christening, 4th August 1982.

Left: The Prince and Princess of Wales at Caernarfon during their tour of Wales, October 1981.

Above: Prince Claus of the Netherlands with Queen Elizabeth II and The Queen Mother at Hampton Court Palace on his state visit, 18th November 1982.

248

Left and Right: The Prince and Princess of Wales with their son Prince William in New Zealand during the royal visit in April 1983.

Left: Prince Edward with Prince Charles and Princess Diana in Wellington during their visit to New Zealand, April 1983.

Right: Prince Harry was born to Charles and Diana in September 1984.

Left and Right: The Prince and Princess of Wales attend a barbecue at Edmonton Park, Edmonton, Alberta, Canada, 30th June 1983. The Princess of Wales wore a stunning 1870s style dress.

Top Left: Prince Charles, Prince William, Prince Harry and Princess Diana, 1985.

Far left: Prince Charles helping a young Prince William down the steps of the aircraft after arriving at Aberdeen airport, August 1984.

Left: Prince Charles with Diana and sons Harry and William at Balmoral, August 1985.

Right: The Prince and Princess of Wales at the march past of British Gulf Troops, London, 21st June 1985.

Above: Prince Charles and Princess Diana meet Pope John Paul II at the Vatican in Rome, 29th April 1985.

Above: Prince Charles and the
Prime Minister Margaret Thatcher
at a reception for the Percent Club
at Number 10 Downing Street,
December 1986.

Left: Queen Elizabeth II at Dunblane Cathedral, Scotland, March 1996. The Queen met with members of the community reeling from the aftershock of the fatal shootings of 16 schoolchildren and their teacher.

Right: The Queen seen here with the Duke of Edinburgh and the Prince and Princess of Wales on the steps of St George's Chapel, Windsor Castle, for the funeral of the Duchess of Windsor, 30th April 1986.

Above: The Queen's 60th birthday celebrations, Buckingham Palace, April 1986. Also pictured are Prince Philip and the newly-engaged couple Prince Andrew and Sarah Ferguson.

Above: Zara Phillips, Seamus Makim, Laura Fellowes and Prince William waiting in Westminster Abbey for the wedding of Prince Andrew and Sarah Ferguson, July 1986

Left: Prince Andrew marries Sarah Ferguson at Westminster Abbey in London, 23rd July 1986. They become the Duke and Duchess of York following the 600-year-old tradition of naming the second son of the reigning monarch.

Right: Prince Andrew and Sarah Ferguson outside Westminster Abbey in London.

Left: Prince Andrew and Sarah Ferguson after their marriage ceremony.

Above: Prince Andrew and Sarah Ferguson kiss on the balcony at Buckingham Palace in front of crowds, 23rd July 1986.

Above: Prince Charles, Princess Diana and Queen Elizabeth II outside Clarence House for the Queen Mother's 87th Birthday, 5th August 1987.

Above: Members of the royal
family at the Remembrance
Service at the Cenotaph in
Whitehall, 8th November 1987.

Left and below: Prince Harry and Prince William at a polo match in Cirencester, 1987.

Right: Prince Harry and Prince William with their parents in September 1987.

Far right: Princess Diana and Prince William watching Polo at Windsor, May 1988.

Left: Prince Charles, Princess Diana, The Duchess of York Sarah Ferguson and The Duke of York Prince Andrew posing for photographers on their skiing holiday at the Swiss resort of Klosters, 17th February 1987.

Above: Prince Charles on his 40th birthday in Birmingham, November 1988.

Right: Prince Charles and Princess Diana on their Far East Tour, November 1989.

Left: The Prince and Princess of Wales visit a synagogue in Toledo during a trip to Spain in April 1987.

Left: Prince Charles with Princes William and Harry, 1988.

Right: Prince Charles and Prince William at Sandringham, January 1988.

Below: Princes William and Harry leaving hospital after visiting the Duchess of York and her daughter Princess Beatrice at Portland Hospital, 1988.

Left: Christening of Princess Beatrice in the Chapel Royal, St James's Palace, attended by Prince Charles, Princess Diana, Prince William and Prince Harry, 20th December 1988.

Above: The Duke and Duchess of York at the christening of their daughter Princess Beatrice, December 1988.

Left: The Prince and Princess of Wales at Victoria Station waiting for the arrival of the Nigerian President for a State Visit, 1989.

Right: Prince Charles with Princess Diana, Prince William and Prince Harry at the wedding of Sir Francis Brooke and Katherine Hussey, 1989.

Left: Sarah Ferguson, the Duchess of York, pictured on the Royal visit to Canada. 31st July 1989.

Right: Queen Elizabeth with Princess Margaret and Princess Diana waiting to greet the Italian president Senior Cossiga, early 1990s.

Left: The Queen Mother standing outside Clarence House on her 90th Birthday to greet well-wishers with her family, 1990.

Right: Prince Harry aged 6.

Below: Princess Eugenie being held by her mother Sarah Ferguson as they leave Portland Hospital, 1990.

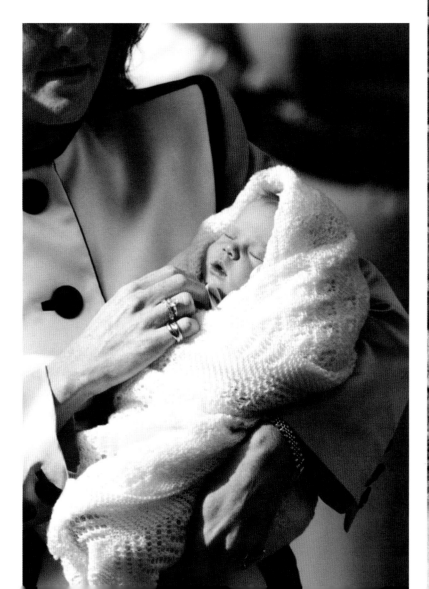

Left: Prince William, aged 7, and Prince Harry, aged 5, return to pre-preparatory Wetherby School after the Easter Break, with their mother Princess Diana, 25th April 1990.

Right: Princess Diana and Prince Charles on a visit to Hungary, May 1990.

Right: Prince Charles, Prince Philip, Prince Harry and Prince William at Sandringham, January 1990.

Above: The christening of Princess
Eugenie in December 1990.

Right: Princess Diana and Prince William
at the Wimbledon Ladies Final, 1991.

Below: Princess Diana during her visit to Pakistan in 1991.

Right: Princess Diana and her children pictured on ski lift in The Alps, Switzerland, 7th April 1991. This was Diana's first ski holiday since her tragic trip with Charles to Klosters three years earlier, when their friend Major Hugh Lindsay was killed.

Left: Princess Diana and Prince Harry laughing and getting soaked on water slide ride, 1992.

Right: The Queen Mother standing outside Clarence House on her 92nd birthday.

Above: Queen Elizabeth II
with her family on the balcony
of Buckingham Palace for
the Trooping of the Colour,
June 1992.

Above: Princess Diana's visit to
Relate Charity, 5th August 1992.

Left: Princess Diana at the Taj Mahal, India, 11th February 1992.

Above: Prince Charles and Princess Diana pictured together during an overseas visit to South Korea, 2nd November 1992. Their marriage was in crisis at this point in time.

Above: Princess Diana with her
two sons on holiday in Austria in
November 1993.

Right: Prince William with his mother Diana, brother Prince Harry and
father Prince Charles before his first day at Eton College Public School,
6th September 1995.

Left: Princess Diana arriving at Versailles, November 1994.

Right: Diana visits a Barnardos home in Paris, France, November 1994.

Above: The Duke and Duchess of York with their two daughters Beatrice and Eugenie at a charity golf tournament in aid of Motor Neurone disease, Wentworth, August 1996.

Left: The Queen Mother meets Prince Andrew in Yorkshire, October 1996.

Right: Sarah Ferguson with her children enjoying the Alps, April 1996.

Above: The Queen Mother with her family
on her 94th birthday, August 1994.

Below: Princess Diana with Madame Chirac – wife of President Chirac – in Paris, 1995.

Right: Princess Anne with war veterans at the 50th Anniversary of D-Day at Omaha Beach, Normandy, France, 6th June 1994.

Left: Princess Diana cuddles a blind child at the Shaukat Khanum Memorial Cancer Hospital, Lahore, February 22, 1996.

Below: Princess Diana with six year old Jamie Poore sitting on her knee during a visit to the children's ward at the Royal Brompton hospital in London, 30th June 1996.

Right: Princess Diana arrives at the Sacred Heart Hospice in Sydney after a three day fundraising trip to Australia, November 1996.

Left: Princes Diana smiling in London for a gala evening sponsored by Chanel, 1st July 1997. Diana was celebrating her 36th birthday.

Right: Princess Diana in a land mine field in Huanbo, Angola, 15th January 1997. She was on a visit to help the Red Cross campaign outlaw landmines worldwide.

PERIGO MINAS!

DANGER MINES

THE HALO TRUST

Left: The body of Diana, Princess of Wales, arrives at RAF Northolt, South Ruislip, from Villacoublay airfield, France, on Sunday 31st August 1997. The Queen's Colour Squadron, based at neighbouring RAF Uxbridge, acted as the bearer party, the flight was also met by the Prime Minister, Tony Blair.

Right: Floral tributes laid outside the gates of Kensington Palace after the death of the Princess of Wales in Paris, August 1997.

Left: Princess Diana's funeral took place on the 6th September 1997. Prince Charles, Prince Harry, Earl Spencer, Prince William and the Duke of Edinburgh watch as the coffin bearing the body of Princess Diana is taken into Westminster Abbey. Millions of mourners lined the streets of central London to watch the funeral procession.

Above: Prince Philip, Prince William, Earl Spencer, Prince Harry and Prince Charles follow behind the cortege that carried Diana's body to Westminster Abbey for the funeral service.

Left: Earl Spencer, Prince William, Prince Harry and Prince Charles in Westminster Abbey during the funeral ceremony for Diana.

Right: The Queen Mother shakes the hand of the Dean of Westminster at Westminster Abbey. Prince Edward stands behind.

Left: Queen Elizabeth II, Prince Philip, Prince Charles, Prince William, Prince Harry and Peter Phillips stop to look at floral tributes left for Princess Diana at the gates of Balmoral Castle.

Right: After attending a private service at Crathie Church, Balmoral Estate, Scotland, Prince Charles looks at floral tributes left for Princess Diana.

Left: Queen Elizabeth II and The Queen Mother at Westminster Abbey for Diana's funeral, September 1997.

Right: Queen Elizabeth II, at Diana's funeral.

CHAPTER 8

The Modern Royal Family

1998–

In 1999, the Queen's youngest son, Edward, married Sophie Rhys-Jones in a relatively informal royal wedding. The couple had decided against a state occasion. The wedding took place in the chapel at Windsor Castle and the guest list numbered under 600 – a vast difference to the 3,500 that attended Charles and Diana's wedding.

With Edward now married, the focus of the media switched to the charming, quiet figure of the Queen Mother as she reached 100 years of age in the year 2000. Celebrations focused on the highlights of her life – she was one of the most popular royals and the stability of the monarchy over the twentieth century can be in part attributed to her presence throughout the whole period.

However, with the passing of the Queen Mother and Princess Margaret in 2002, the natural generational shift of a family happened – the Queen's children and grandchildren had well and truly become the focal point of the royal family. Their lives had been documented by the media from birth, and many of those alive in Britain now feel they have grown up with either the Queen's children or her older grandchildren: William, Harry, Philip, Zara, Beatrice and Eugenie.

William and Harry were educated at Eton College, and both young royals then took a gap year aged 18. William went on to study at St Andrews University and then served in the British Armed Forces as a search and rescue pilot. Harry also joined the British Army and went on to serve in Afghanistan. Both boys take after their mother by undertaking lots of charitable work on the side of their official royal duties.

In 2005, nine years after his divorce from Diana, Charles married Camilla Parker Bowles. The Church of England and the Queen gave their consent to a civil ceremony followed by religious prayer. Charles had known Camilla for over 30 years and their friendship was common knowledge, but it took years to for Charles to gain the full approval of his family and country. Camilla is now an established member of the royal family and is seen to be a great support to her husband as he fulfills his duty as heir to the throne.

Left: Prince Charles with his sons Prince William and Prince Harry
on the ski slopes in Klosters, April 2000.

Weddings and births mark changing points within any family, and none more than Prince William's marriage to Catherine Middleton. William and Kate met at St Andrews University in Scotland. Much thanks to the legacy of his mother, William was afforded privacy from the media during his time at university and their romance was quietly allowed to blossom. This was vastly different to the public scrutiny that Charles and Diana had experienced.

After a brief separation, William asked Kate to marry him in 2010 and the build up to the wedding in April 2011 was feverous. The Queen, on advice from her government, declared a public holiday for the day and the wedding ceremony was televised around the world. Kate wore a dress designed by Sarah Burton for Alexander McQueen and her engagement ring was the one Charles had given to Diana 30 years previously. This young couple immediately took over the role of figureheads for the royal brand and boosted the interest and approval of the monarchy once again.

In 2013 Prince George Alexander Louis was born, and he became third in line to the throne. For the first time since 1894 a monarch and three heirs were alive at the same time. A 300-year-old succession law was also changed at this time to allow first-born daughters to retain their heir apparent status even if they have younger brothers. Princess Charlotte Elizabeth Diana, William and Kate's second child, was born in 2015 and the world waits to see what this new generation of royals will bring to the monarchy.

Left: Charles, Edward and Andrew arriving at the wedding of Edward's marriage to Sophie Rhys-Jones at St George's Chapel in Windsor, 1999.

Right: Prince Edward and Sophie leave the chapel after their wedding.

Left: Edward and his bride Sophie Rhys-Jones wave from an open top carriage following the wedding service.

Below: Sophie Rhys Jones, Prince Edward, Princess Anne and husband Tim Taylor with Queen Elizabeth II watching the Trooping of the Colour from Buckingham Palace, June 1999.

Right: Princess Anne taking part in the Trooping of the Colour in June 1999.

Left: Peter Phillips, the son of Princess Anne, at his School Rugby Sevens played at Kingston Park, Newcastle on 5th May 1996.

Above: Zara Phillips, daughter of Princess Anne, August 1998.

Right: The Queen Mother with Princess Margaret sitting in a carriage at Royal Ascot, June 1996.

Left: Queen Elizabeth, The Queen Mother, with The Duke of Edinburgh, during her 100th birthday celebrations in London, 4th August 2000.

Above: The Queen Mother on the balcony of Buckingham Place with members of her family.

Above: The Queen Mother is greeted by the Lord Mayor of London and her grandson and great-grandsons Prince Charles, Prince William and Prince Harry at the side entrance of St Paul's Cathedral where a national thanksgiving service was held in honour of her 100th birthday.

Above: Prince Charles, with sons
Prince William and Prince Harry,
on Buckingham Palace balcony at
The Queen Mother's 100th birthday
celebrations, August 2000.

Left: Prince Charles with his grandmother on her birthday.

Right: Prince Harry and Prince Charles attend a memorial service in London for the victims of the September 11th terrorist attacks in America, 2001.

Above: The Queen Mother on her 101st birthday watched by Princess Margaret, in a wheelchair, Prince Charles, Prince William and Prince Harry, August 2001.

Right: The Queen Mother passed away on the 30th March 2002. Here, Prince Philip salutes at her funeral as Prince Charles follows the coffin to Westminster Abbey, April 2002.

Left: The Queen Mother's Funeral,
April 2002.

Above: The body of the Queen
Mother arrives at Windsor,
entering the Castle via the King
Henry VIII Gate.

Above: The funeral of Princess Margaret at St George's Chapel, Windsor, February 2002. Prince Andrew, Prince William, Prince Charles, Prince Harry, Peter Phillips, Prince Edward, Captain Timothy Lawrence, Sophie Countess of Wessex and Princess Anne.

Right: The Duke and Duchess of York with their daughter Princess Beatrice and Sarah's sister Jane, pictured after the church service for the funeral of Sarah and Jane's father, Major Ron Ferguson, March 2003.

Far left: Prince Harry covered in mud, after playing in the Eton Wall game, November 2002.

Left: Prince Harry is Parade Commander of the 48 strong guard of honour at the combined cadet forces Tattoo at Eton College, May 2003.

Right: Prince William signs the Book of Condolence for the London bombing victims at the British Consulate in Auckland, New Zealand, July 2005.

Left: Queen Elizabeth II on her way to open the Churchill Museum on the day that her son Charles, the Prince of Wales, announced his forthcoming marriage to Camilla Parker Bowles, October 2004.

Above: Prince Harry and Prince William after the wedding ceremony at Windsor Guildhall, between their father Prince Charles and Camilla Parker Bowles, 9th April 2005. Also pictured are Camilla's children Tom Parker Bowles and Laura Parker Bowles (obscured).

Far left: The civil wedding of Prince Charles and Camilla Parker Bowles at Windsor Guildhall on 9th April 2005.

Left: Camilla and Charles arriving for their blessing at St George's Chapel, Windsor.

Above: Prince Charles and Camilla Parker Bowles pictured meeting the public after leaving the chapel service at Windsor.

Above: Prince William and Prince Harry at Sandhurst Royal Military Academy after The Sovereign's Parade that marked the completion of Prince Harry's Officer training.

Above: Prince Harry, second from right, grins and his grandmother Queen Elizabeth II smiles, as she inspects the Sovereign's Parade at the Royal Military Academy in Sandhurst, 12th April 2006. Prince Harry was one of the cadets passing out as a commissioned officer, and went on to join the Blues and Royals, part of the Household Cavalry, and one of Britain's oldest army regiments.

Left: William and Harry at their helicopter training base RAF Shawbury, Shropshire, June 2009.

Below: Prince Charles visiting Seaton Delaval Hall, September 2009.

Right: Kate Middleton in the Royal box at Cheltenham racecourse, 13th March 2007.

Left: Prince William and Kate Middleton at Cheltenham, 13th March 2007.

Right: Prince William and his fiancée Kate Middleton joined Prince Harry in London to sign a book of condolence for the victims of New Zealand's earthquake, February 2011.

Left: Crowds of people wave British flags as they wait for Prince William and his wife Catherine, Duchess of Cambridge, to appear on the balcony of Buckingham Palace on their wedding day, 29th April 2011.

Right: Prince William arrives with Prince Harry at Westminster Abbey for his wedding to Catherine Middleton. William is wearing the ceremonial uniform of a Colonel of the Irish Guards, Prince Harry wears the uniform of a Captain of the Blues and Royals.

Left: The procession containing the happy couple makes its way back to Buckingham Palace following the ceremony at Westminster Abbey.

Right: Prince Andrew, Princesses Eugenie and Beatrice leave Westminster Abbey after the wedding of Britain's Prince William and Kate Middleton. Beatrice wore a taupe Valentino Haute Couture dress and matching coat. Eugenie wore a blue and green Vivienne Westwood suit.

Left: Prince Charles, Prince Phillip, Camilla the Duchess of Cornwall and The Queen leave the Abbey after the royal wedding.

Above: Kate Middleton arrives at Westminster Abbey with her sister Pippa Middleton, her maid of honour, holding the train of her dress.

Above: Queen Elizabeth II and
Prince Philip leave Westminster
Abbey following the wedding
ceremony in a royal carriage.

Above: Prince Harry waves to the crowd with a young bridesmaid and page boy as they make the journey by carriage procession to Buckingham Palace following the ceremony at Westminster Abbey.

Left: Prince William and his bride, the Duchess of Cambridge emerge from Westminster Abbey, following the ceremony.

Right: Kate and William leave Westminster Abbey after their wedding.

Above: Catherine, Duchess of Cambridge, and Prince William travel the processional route from Westminster Abbey to Buckingham Place in the 1902 State Landau carriage, following their wedding ceremony.

Right: A street party for the Royal Wedding of Prince William and Catherine Middleton in Cardiff, 29th April, 2011.

The newly married couple share a kiss on the balcony at Buckingham Palace as they are joined by bridesmaids, page boys and family members. Left to right, Michael Middleton, Carole Middleton, Prince Charles holding bridesmaid Eliza Lopes, Camilla Duchess of Cornwall, Lady Louise Windsor, Grace van Cutsem, Margarita Armstrong-Jones, Tom Pettifer, William Lowther-Pinkerton, Queen Elizabeth II, Prince Philip, maid of honour Pippa Middleton and best man Prince Harry.

Left: Prince William and his new wife leave Buckingham Palace in an Aston Martin for the short drive to Clarence House.

Below: The Duchess of Cambridge at a gala dinner at the Royal Albert Hall to celebrate the country's Olympic and Paralympic athletes, 11th May 2012.

Right: The Duke and Duchess of Cambridge at the Foundation Polo Challenge at the Santa Barbara Racquet and Polo Club, California, 9th July 2011. The event benefits the American Friends of the Foundation of Prince William and Prince Harry, a charity which supports disadvantaged children, conservation and sustainable development, veterans and military families.

Above: The Queen celebrated her Diamond Jubilee in 2012 and members of the royal family watched the Diamond Jubilee pageant on the River Thames in London on the 1st June.

Above: Camilla, Duchess of Cornwall, Prince Charles, Queen Elizabeth II, Prince William, Catherine, Duchess of Cambridge and Prince Harry wave to the crowds from Buckingham Palace during the Diamond Jubilee on 5th June, 2012.

Left: Queen Elizabeth II on the occasion of her Diamond Jubilee.

Right: Queen Elizabeth II is joined by other members of the royal family for the Trooping of the Colour Ceremony on the 15th June 2013.

Left: The Queen attends the Order of the Garter service with Prince William, 17th June 2013.

Right: The Duke and Duchess of Cambridge leave the Lindo Wing at St Mary's Hospital, Paddington, with their new born son Prince George Alexander Louis. He was born on the 22nd July 2013.

Left: The Duke and Duchess of Cambridge, along with Prince George, arrive in Wellington, New Zealand ahead of their tour of New Zealand and Australia. They were greeted by traditional Maori dancers.

Below: The eight-month-old Prince George at Government House in Wellington at a special playgroup arranged in his honour, April 2014.

Right: The family arrive at Sydney Airport on an Australian Airforce 737 aircraft on 16th April 2014. This was their first official trip overseas with their son, Prince George of Cambridge.

Left: Prince Charles and Camilla attended the 150th birthday of the historic highland games in Ballater's Monaltrie Park, Scotland, 14th August 2014.

Above: Prince William, Camilla, Duchess of Cornwall, Prince Charles and Prince Harry at the Queen Elizabeth II Olympic Park during the Invictus Games Opening Ceremony on 10th September 2014.

The Duke and Duchess of Cornwall and Prince Harry attend London's Tower of London for the *Blood Swept Lands and Seas of Red* poppies installation on 5th August 2015.

Above: Catherine, Duchess of Cambridge, pictured at Barlby Primary School in London on the 15th January 2015 to officially name the Clore Art Room.

Above: Catherine, Duchess of Cambridge, and Prince William pictured on a royal visit to urban youth charity XLP in Gipsy Hill, London on the 27th March 2015. The couple were presented with a babygrow for their second child.

Left: Prince William brings Prince George to the Lindo Wing at St Mary's Hospital on the 2nd May 2015 to meet his newborn sister.

Above: The Duke and Duchess of Cambridge with their new baby daughter, Princess Charlotte Elizabeth Diana. She was born on the 2nd May 2005.

Above: Prince William with his newborn daughter.

Right: Princess Charlotte with her mother.

Left: The Duchess of Cambridge holds Princess Charlotte after her christening at St Mary Magdalene Church, Sandringham, 5th July 2015. The Queen, Prince Philip, Camilla, Duchess of Cornwall, Prince William and Prince George surround her.

The Coventry Evening Telegraph

LAST EDITION

No. 19,314 [63rd Year].　　　TUESDAY, JUNE 2, 1953.　　　TWOPENCE.

YOUR UNDOUBTED QUEEN

Right: The front page of *The Coventry Evening Telegraph* on the day of Queen Elizabeth II's coronation ceremony. Over 60 years later she matches Queen Victoria's epic reign and status as an unforgettable monarch.

First published in 2015 by New Holland Publishers Pty Ltd
London • Sydney • Auckland

The Chandlery Unit 009, 50 Westminster Bridge Road, London SE1 7QY, United Kingdom
1/66 Gibbes Street, Chatswood, NSW 2067, Australia
5/39 Woodside Ave, Northcote, Auckland 0627, New Zealand

www.newhollandpublishers.com

A record of this book is held at the British Library and the National Library of Australia.

ISBN 9781742577548

Managing Director: Fiona Schultz
Publisher: Alan Whiticker
Project Editor: Anna Brett
Proofreader: Jessica McNamara
Designer: Andrew Davies
Production Director: Olga Dementiev
Printer: Toppan Leefung Printing Limited

10 9 8 7 6 5 4 3 2 1

Keep up with New Holland Publishers on Facebook
www.facebook.com/NewHollandPublishers

mirrorpix